WILD AMERICA

OPOSSUM

By Lee Jacobs

**BLACKBIRCH®
PRESS**

THOMSON

GALE

San Diego • Detroit • New York • San Francisco • Cleveland • New Haven, Conn. • Waterville, Maine • London • Munich

THOMSON
——— ★ ———
GALE

For Marla, who
has a soft spot
for opossums!

Photo Credits: Cover, pages 4, 9, 20, 22 © Thomas Kitchin & Victoria Hurst; pages 3, 8, 23 © Bruce Glassman; page 5 © Corel Corporation; pages 6, 7, 10, 11, 13, 14-15, 18-19, 21 © CORBIS; pages 10, 16-17 © Alden M. Johnson, California Academy of Sciences

LIBRARY OF CONGRESS CATALOGING-IN-PUBLICATION DATA

Jacobs, Lee.
 Opossum / by Lee Jacobs.
  p. cm. — (Wild America habitats series)
 Summary: Discusses the body, food, mating and living habits of the opossum, and its interaction with humans.
 Includes bibliographical references and index.
  ISBN 1-56711-570-5 (hardback : alk. paper)
 1. Opossums—Juvenile literature. [1. Opossums.] I. Title. II. Series.
 QL737.M34 J34 2003
 599.2'76—dc21   2002010366

Printed in China
10 9 8 7 6 5 4 3 2 1

Contents

Introduction

The opossum is one of the oldest living mammals in the world. Opossums have been on Earth for 70 to 80 million years. That means they lived at the same time as Tyrannosaurus rex!

Opossums are a kind of mammal called marsupials. They belong to the order Marsupialia. Like all mammals, marsupials give birth to live young. What makes marsupials unique are the pouches that females have on the outside of their bodies.

There are nearly 270 different species of marsupials in the world. Most—such as kangaroos, koalas, and wallabies—live in Australia, New Guinea, and islands in the Pacific Ocean. About 75 species of marsupials are opossums that belong to the family Didelphidae. They live mainly in Central and South America. The Virginia opossum makes its home in North America.

Opossums are the only marsupials found in North America.

In fact, it is the only marsupial found in North America! It lives in more than two-thirds of the United States, including the Pacific Coast, the Great Lakes region, the Southeast, and New England. The Virginia opossum also lives in parts of Mexico and Canada.

The name *opossum* comes from the Algonquian word *apasum*. It means "white animal." English explorer Captain John Smith, who settled Jamestown, Virginia, in 1607, was the first to use the word opossum. People today often shorten the name and say, "possum." That is a mistake. Real possums live in Australia and are not at all related to the Virginia opossum.

Opossums are members of a group of mammals called marsupials. Other members of this group include the koala (top), the kangaroo (bottom, left), and the wallaby (bottom, right).

The Opossum's Environment

Opossums live in a wide range of habitats, including farmlands, woodlands, and even neighborhoods. They usually live in an area of about 95 acres (40 ha), but they often wander farther when they search for food. Opossums are not very picky about where they live, as long as there is food and water nearby. Although all animals must drink water to survive, opossums also like it because they love to swim.

Opossums live in woodlands, as well as many other types of habitats.

Opossums are ground-dwellers, but they are excellent climbers, too. Trees provide opossums with food, as well as places to escape predators (animals that hunt and eat other animals).

Within its home range, an opossum makes several nests, or dens. Some may be high in trees, but others may be close to the ground in tree hollows. Opossums also make homes in the abandoned nests or burrows of other animals, or even in rocky openings. They line their nests with twigs, grasses, and leaves.

Opossums often make nests in burrows that other animals abandon.

The Opossum Body

An opossum's body is long and slender. It has a thick, soft, furry undercoat with a topcoat of long, coarse hairs. The topcoat helps protect it from wet weather. Opossums range in color from grayish white to reddish brown. Some opossums that live in southern regions can be blackish in color. Like all marsupials, female opossums have a pouch to carry their young. Virginia opossums are the largest opossums. They weigh between 4 and 14 pounds (2 to 6 kg). The length of the body ranges from 13 to 20 inches (33 to 51 cm). The long tail adds an extra 10 to 21 inches (25 to 53 cm).

Opossums have triangular white faces and large, rounded, furless ears that are rimmed with black. Their eyes are also ringed with black markings. Opossums have excellent night vision, as well as keen senses of hearing and smell. Their noses are long, pink, and pointed. They are not covered in fur. Sensitive whiskers called vibrissae aid their sense of touch.

Opposite page: An opossum's topcoat of long, course hairs helps protect it from bad weather.
Inset: Opossums have long, triangle-shaped faces.

Their large mouths can open wide to eat a variety of foods, as well as to show off their sharp teeth. Opossums have 50 teeth—more than any other North American land mammal! The undersides of an opossum's paws are lined with soft skin. Each front paw has 5 long toes with claws, and each back paw has 4 clawed toes. The claws are too short to let opossums dig very well. The back paws have a fifth thumb-like toe. An opossum uses these special toes to help it climb and grasp objects.

Opossums also have tails that are designed to grab onto things. These are called prehensile tails. Opossums are the only North American mammals that have them. Many people think opossums hang upside down by their tails, but that is not true.

Above: Opossums have very sharp teeth. Their ability to open their mouths wide allows them to eat many kinds of food.
Below: Sharp claws help opossums climb trees.

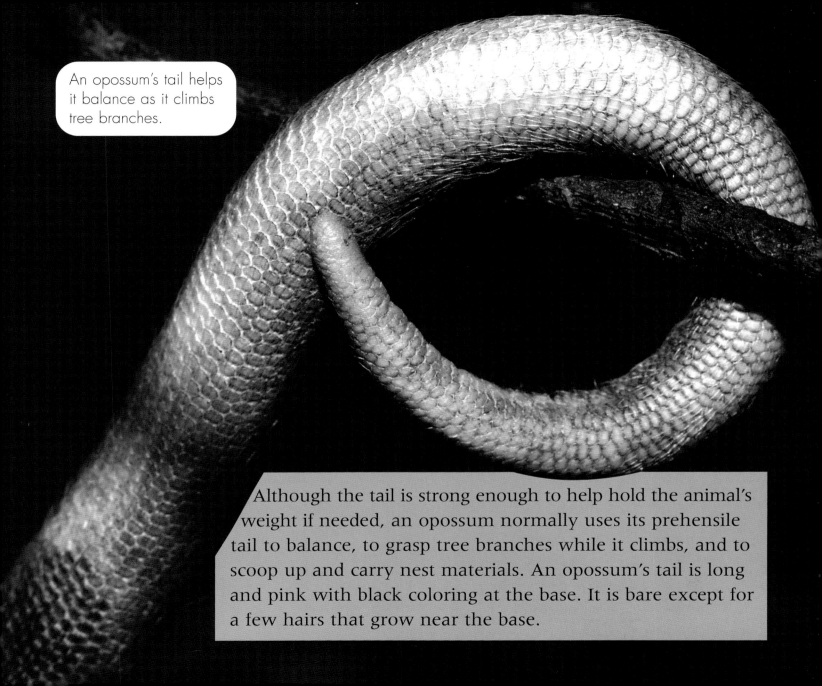

An opossum's tail helps it balance as it climbs tree branches.

Although the tail is strong enough to help hold the animal's weight if needed, an opossum normally uses its prehensile tail to balance, to grasp tree branches while it climbs, and to scoop up and carry nest materials. An opossum's tail is long and pink with black coloring at the base. It is bare except for a few hairs that grow near the base.

Social Life

Like other marsupials, opossums are nocturnal animals. This means they sleep during the day and are active at night. Opossums prefer to live on their own. They are not very territorial. They do not mind if they have to share space with other animals. Although a female opossum may sometimes let another female into her nest, males and females never sleep in the same dens.

Because opossums do not run very fast, they have adapted other ways to protect themselves. They are generally quiet animals, but they will growl or hiss if threatened. An opossum will bare its sharp teeth to scare off a predator. It may also drool to make itself look sick, since a diseased animal is not a good choice for a meal.

The saying "playing 'possum" refers to one very effective way opossums protect themselves: They play dead. They curl up on the ground and stay perfectly still to discourage predators, such as dogs, cats, coyotes, or great horned owls. Most animals will not attack a dead animal, so the predator usually gives up and leaves. An opossum can play dead for a few minutes or for as long as several hours. When it plays dead, an opossum does not just pretend. Its body actually sends a substance into the bloodstream that causes the muscles to contract. This effect does not wear off until the danger is gone.

Opossums have one other trick to ward off an attacker. Like skunks, they have glands that can release a foul-smelling liquid. Although opossums cannot spray the liquid the way skunks can, its odor is bad enough to make an enemy run away.

When an enemy threatens, an opossum plays dead. They may remain in this state for several hours.

13

Hunting

Like all nocturnal animals, opossums hunt at night. Their keen hearing, eyesight, and sense of smell help them function well in the dark.

Opossums can live in many different habitats because they adapt to their environment and eat whatever foods are available. Their diet consists of a wide range of foods, including fruit, nuts, insects, snails, frogs, crayfish, small rodents, and bird eggs. Some opossums that live in the tropical climates of Central and South America eat mainly fruit and nectar. North America's Virginia opossum, on the other hand, is omnivorous. This means it eats both animals and plants. Some opossums will even eat carrion (dead animals) and any other food they might find as they rummage through neighborhood garbage cans. They are also able to store fat to help them live through times when food is hard to find.

An opossum feeds on a dead rabbit. Opossums will eat almost anything they find.

The average opossum litter is made up of 8 or 9 babies.

The Mating Game

A male opossum is called a jack, and a female is called a jill. Males and females only pair off when it is time to mate, and males do not help raise the young. Breeding season can begin in December and last until October, but most opossums mate between January and August. Many females have 2 litters per year.

Although opossums often share territory with other animals, they scent-mark their home range during breeding season. To do this, they wet their fur with saliva, then rub against trees and other spots in the area where they live.

When jacks compete for a female, they often make clicking sounds at each other. They make this same sound to attract females.

Female opossums are pregnant for only about 11 to 13 days. Just before a Virginia opossum has her babies, she makes a soft leafy nest in a safe place, such as a fallen log, tree hollow, or abandoned burrow.

Babies

Opossum babies are called joeys. (The babies of kangaroos and koalas, two other types of marsupials, are also called joeys.) An opossum may have more than 20 babies in 1 litter, but the average litter has 8 or 9 babies. Joeys are extremely small at birth. They weigh less than 1 ounce (28 g) and are only about 0.5 inches (1 cm) long. Many of these newborns together could fit in 1 teaspoon. The babies are born deaf, blind, and furless. They depend completely on their mother.

As soon as they are born, these tiny pink babies have to make a difficult climb through their mother's fur to reach her pouch. There, they will nurse and grow in safety. To make their journey a bit easier, the mother opossum licks a path through her hair. If a baby loses its way and runs into a patch of dry hair, it knows it has to change its course a bit to get back on track. The babies have special claws on their front toes, designed just for this trip. The claws fall off soon after the babies arrive in the mother's cozy pouch.

Joeys are born blind, deaf, and hairless. They are completely dependent on their mother for survival.

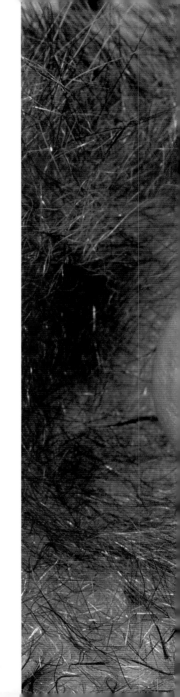

In order to survive, a baby must make it to the pouch and then latch on to one of the mother's 13 teats, or nipples. If a joey does not attach to a teat, it will die. If a mother has more than 13 babies, the ones that cannot nurse do not live long.

Joeys nurse inside the pouch for 2 to 4 months. Their eyes open after 55 to 70 days. Around this time, some of the babies start to leave the pouch for short periods of time.

Once they leave the pouch for good, joeys travel on their mother's back for another 2 months. To stay on, they grasp her fur with their claws and teeth. As they watch their mother search for food and avoid predators, they learn important survival skills.

At 4 to 6 months old, a joey weighs 10 to 18 ounces (284 to 510 g) and is about 7 to 11 inches (18 to 28 cm) long, not including its tail.

Opossum babies travel on their mother's back until they can take care of themselves.

The babies are ready to go off on their own around this time, although some stay with their mother until they are about a year old. This is a long time, considering that opossums usually live only a year or two in the wild.

If a mother with babies on her back is threatened by a predator, she may hiss or growl, but she will not play dead. To do so would put her babies in too much danger.

Mother and babies have special ways to communicate with each other. If a baby opossum is separated from its mother, it makes a sneezing sound to attract her attention. In turn, the mother makes a clicking sound to signal to her lost joey.

Joeys may stay with their mother until they are a year old.

21

Opossums and Humans

In the early 1800s, Virginia opossums were found only in Panama, southern Mexico, and a few parts of the United States. Because these opossums can easily learn to live around humans, though, their range has spread over the past 200 years. Opossums are hunted by several wild predators. Humans and pet dogs also pose a major danger. Some people hunt opossums for sport. In many parts of the South, they are killed for food. Cars also kill a large number of opossums.

Many opossums are killed by cars and other vehicles.

Some people think opossums are pests because they sometimes raid chicken coops and cornfields. Opossums can be helpful to humans, however. They eat the snails in gardens, but do not disturb the plants. They eat all kinds of bugs, including crickets, cockroaches, and beetles. This helps keep the insect population down. Opossums also hunt small rodents such as mice and rats, which carry diseases that can be harmful to humans. Opossums greatly benefit neighborhoods as they get rid of pests and clean up rotten fruit that has fallen to the ground. To have an opossum occasionally eat pet food that has been left out for the night seems a small price to pay, considering that these animals can be a town's most dependable clean-up crew.

Opossums are helpful to humans in certain ways. They eat pests in gardens, and small rodents that carry harmful diseases.

Glossary

carrion dead or decaying animals

jack a male opossum

jill a female opossum

joey a baby opossum

marsupial a group of animals in which the female has a pouch that is used to carry young after they are born

nocturnal an animal that sleeps during the day and is active at night

omnivore an animal that eats both plants and other animals

predator an animal that hunts other animals for food

prehensile adapted to grasp, hold, or wrap around things

vibrissae sensitive whiskers of an animal

For Further Reading

Books

Crofford, Emily. *Opossum (Wildlife: Habits & Habitat)*. Parsippany, NJ: Crestwood House, 1990.

Kalman, Bobbie. *What Is a Mammal?* New York: Crabtree Publishing, 1998.

Lee, Sandra. *Opossums (Naturebooks)*. Chanhassen, MN: Child's World, 1998.

Walker, Sally. *Opossum at Sycamore Road (Smithsonian Backyard)*. Norwalk, CT: Soundprints, 1997.

Index